Trials of Life

Also by Donald W. Grant

Poetry

Shades of Life
Echoes of Life
Silence of Life
Reflections of Life

Non-Fiction

M.A.G.A.: Making America Go Awry

Trials of Life

A Collection of Poems

By
Donald W. Grant

DC
D2C Perspectives

Table of Contents

To my wife, my soulmate, without whom I would never survive the trials of life

White Privilege

The less,
Having less even more.
The more,
Unhappy demanding more
....White privilege

Life savers
stretched beyond belief.
The more,
Whimpering for relief
....White privilege

Men and a few women,
Mostly old and gray,
Arguing about who and
Just how much to pay
....White privilege

Old and frail
Unable to survive.
Bean counters more worried
About coins
Not who stays
....White privilege

The dead,
Too many to just bury.

Ignorant souls
Armed, arrogant, and angry
….White privilege

A virus causing the carnage
A virus called…White privilege

The Blame Game

Shakespeare asked us,
"What's in a name?"
Yet then he says, to a
Montague, a Capulat is profane.

Regardless of what we give a name,
The essence of that thing
Is still the same.

Today, more than ever, we
seem to be playing the name game.

Labels are used to place blame,
To remind us we are not the same

Caucasion, Black, Asian,
Latino, or Native American.
Labels to put us in boxes,
Supposedly to easier understand.

But instead, used to promote hate.
This was not what our fate
was meant to be, all are equal,
all meant to be free.

As long as we allow the misuse
of these names,

We will never take responsibility
for our actions, for there will
always be someone else to blame.

The Blood of Christ

"The blood of Christ will protect me."
Ignorance disguised as faith.

Faith in the unseen to
Protect from the unseen.

Blind faith that could lead to death,
Not death of the ignorant, but
Death of the innocent.

The right to believe
Trumping the right to live.

"Praise to the Lord," you say,
But to you He turns a deaf ear.

The love of Christ rejects you.
The blood of Christ
Cannot protect you
From yourself.

The Boy Who Wanted To Be King

Ages before the word became flesh,
A people were unjustly suppressed.
Pharaoh refused to hear the cries of distress.
It took seven plagues for him to acquiesce.

Thirty-three years after the birth of the Word,
Pilate decided to ignore what he heard.
Washing his hands, failing to act was absurd.
He had the power, yet he failed to save the Word.

Two thousand years and a score more
since the Word was crucified,
A new boy wanting to be King has arrived.
Facing a plague and a people restless,
He has done nothing but lie.
His inaction has caused the sickness
to spread, his inaction has caused many to die.

History has not been kind to
the King of Egypt, nor Pontus Pilate.
The new boy-king who so wanted
accolades, will be seen as the worst,
as history writes it.

The New Death

Death has always been a lonely journey.
We have always stepped into the void alone.

To those left behind, we become just a memory.
Those left behind leaving words unsaid, regretfully.

While death is still a constant, things have changed.

Many not only die alone, but slide toward death alone.
Loved ones now say goodbye over the phone.

No one is there to hold your hand,
To tell you those left will be alright.

No one there to pray for your soul,
To give you your last rite.

No one will be able to place flowers on your grave.
Only your ashes will remain for your loved ones to
sprinkle or save.

The New Normal

"Play ball!"
A sound falling on deaf ears.
There is no one here,
No one in the stands,
No one in the tiers.

The game is about to start,
The anthem is about to play.
There is no one here,
No one to place a hand
Over their heart.

"Good evening, your table is ready,
And as you can see, there aren't that many.
Each one set at least six feet apart,
Would you like a drink to start?"

"Your server's name is June, and
She will be with you soon.
She is putting on gloves and a mask.
If you need anything else, just ask."

"Welcome aboard, and as you can see,
No one is here except the pilot and me.
Take any seat, there seems to be plenty.
No one is here except you and your family."

"The doctor will see you now,
Just log in and turn on video chat.
He will ask you your symptoms, and
We hope they are minor and not
more than that."

The hospital halls are still full of gurneys,
Doctors and nurses still moving in a flurry.
The morgue is also still at capacity.
A refrigerator truck still takes the dead
on their last journey.

The manicured cemeteries are now full,
No room for any more ornate headstones.
The bodies now fill mass graves
At least, no one is buried alone.
This is the new normal, at least for now.

Hopefully some lessons have been learned
And we will all be better off,
at least for those still alive,
Maybe the planet will now
have a chance to survive.

Through Her Eyes

The playground is empty
The swings silent.

No toys in the sandbox,
No monkeys on the bars.

Police tape wrapped
Around the slide

As if a murder had taken place.
Did someone die?

She stands in the grass
Off to the side.

"Why?" She asks, "Can I
Not go down the slide?"

Her world has been
Turned upside down,

Too young to understand
What is really going down.

A tear emerges from my eye
To see the loss of what she had,

But it is my heart that breaks
When I hear her say, "I'm sad."

Utilitarianism

Who decides who will live?
Who decides who will die?

How many lives are we
Willing to sacrifice for
The common good?

When did your desire
For a Happy Meal
Become worth more
Than my right to live.

When did your desire
To keep your body fit
Become worth more
Than my right to life.

When did your pleasure
Become worth more
Than my ability to breathe.

Greed now trumps
My right to exist.

Nature

The tide continues to
Roll in and out,
Caressing the sand that
Struggles to hold on.

Sanderlings dart back
And forth seeking morsels
As the water recedes.

Sea gulls still gather,
Fighting over what people
Have left behind,
Each claiming, "Mine, mine."

Seals and otters glide
Through the surf,
Unaware of the chaos
And pelicans still soar.

People struggle to survive,
Fighting an invisible death
As nature simply rolls along,
Like the tide caressing the shore.

Ode To Toilet Paper

I am sorry I took you for granted.

You have always been there for me.

Knowing you were there made me

Use you more often than I should.

At times I requested too much of you,

Secure in assuming you would last.

Now you are gone, and I cry,

Willing to pay any price just to hold you again.

Out of Balance

Visibility removed as man
Darts from point A to point B
(Man here referring to human kind).

Visibility restored as man
Is forced to be still, to stop
(Man is an easier word to rhyme).

Concrete and blacktop haphazardly
Forcing wildlife to shady corners.
Wild animals now stepping from the shade
Onto the blacktop as the concrete
Structures stand empty.

Birds no longer sucked into
The turbines of winged steel
As the metal birds no longer fly.

The extraction of crushed dinosaurs
Ceased as the need has been curtailed.
The greed, the lies, the falsehood of caring,
Now exposed by truth, by the need for sharing

The arrogance of civilization
Brought to its knees by one realization
In the battle nature versus man, it will always be
Nature that has the upper hand.

Outbreak

Death being faced alone,
No one to comfort you,
No one holding your hand.

Death becoming a choice,
Who lives, who dies,
Unable to save them all.

Numbers now exponential,
Too many to care for,
Life now reduced to statistics.

Ignorance now a disease
As deadly as any bacteria
As contagious as any virus.

Lives needlessly lost
Precautions failed to be taken,
No one to hold responsible.

Pandemic

Walls closing in,
Anxiety compressing the air,
Instability fueling the unknown.

Truth muddled in confusion,
Facts seemingly irretrievable,
Information no longer reliable.

Past failures to blame,
Future reality a fog,
Present moments on shaky ground.

Death knocking on every door,
No blood able to repel,
Life once sure now uncertain.

Resisting

Protesters are clogging the streets
Demanding their right to speak out,
Wanting to be able to get haircuts,
Manicures, food that is not takeout.

Some of them wave rebel flags,
Some of them are armed
They're not worried about the virus,
Believing all this is a false alarm

Willing to take their chances,
Believing they are immune.
Sadly, they could be infected,
Which would make them
change their tune.

Believing their right to congregate
Trumps others right to life.
Not caring if their action causes you to die,
An act that will be judged in the afterlife.

So while the majority shelter in place
Maintaining social distancing,
The ignorant minority just
keep on resisting.

Restoration

Humanity at a crossroads,
Nature forcing a new direction.

Man failed to be concerned,
Nature could no longer wait.

Air and water compromised,
Plastic covering the earth.

Creation begging for relief,
Man ignoring in disbelief.

Nature cries enough,
Bringing man to his knees.

The new direction now clear,
Only one road left to follow.

Chaos

Silent, invisible, patiently waiting,
Waiting to seep into the soul.

Seeping into the soul of wellness,
A wellness that moves the air.

The air that moves quietly in and out,
In and out now meeting resistance.

Resistance that seeks to silence life,
Life now on the edge, fighting.

Fighting to maintain, to not die,
Dying is the goal of that which is

Silent, invisible, patiently waiting.

Confused

There is a song with the lines:
"First you say you do and then you don't
then you say you will and then you won't"
So here we sit confused.

Do we mask or not mask?
Do we allow small groups or no groups?
Do we go outside or stay inside?
Is this a hoax or a pandemic?

So much information and misinformation.
At a time when we need answers
We have more questions.
At a time when we need leadership
We get a buffoon.

When we need support we get politics.
In the best country in the world
We have the worst response.

Confusion, delusion, no resolution,
Maybe it is time for a revolution.

Acceptance

We have always known most were corrupt,
The problem was most of us did not care.
After all, their greed and their corruption
Had little to do with how or who we are.

It took a black man to finally begin
to expose the truth of just who we had
put in charge, of just how deep
corruption had taken root, of just
how out of touch leadership had become.

And then came the epitome of evil.
Pick a word: narcissist, sociopath,
misogynist, creep, racist, ignorant,
egomaniac, bigot, all of which are
incorporated into one dark soul.

The truth of how things are and
how things work, came smashing into
our reality, and most of us were stunned,
caught off guard, blinking in disbelief.
As Jorie Graham would write, we thought
things were as bad as x, when actually they
were as bad as y.

Now no matter how bad the lies, how bad
The deception, how bad the deflection,

we still do not get it, we still think things
will change. We have become numb
to abnormal.

Now as thousands die,
we shrug our shoulders
And say, "Oh, well, what can we do!"

Contemplation

The sun was still waiting to make an appearance.

The room was cold, as night still had it in its grip.

Pressures of life suffocating and unsurmountable.

Silence.

No sound but the slow inhalation
and exhalation of a breath.

Choice had now become clear, life or death.

Trembling hands held the answer,
All that was needed was courage.

Tears fell as the mind said
Goodbye to all that was before.

The decision had been made the life was to be taken.

From nowhere a sound, another
Human too close to not hear.

Decision now dismissed, perhaps
To be resurrected another day.

Crying Wolf

He tried to warn us,
The boy-wonder,
Five years ahead
Of the rest of us.

His cry fell on deaf ears
But his words have come to pass.
Had we listened our graves
Would not be full, but
Sadly, our leader is a dumb ass.

Truth, facts, science,
Knowledge from those who know,
Replaced by hunches, rumors,
Boldface lies, all for show.

One man's popularity
more important
Than reality.
One man's truth
Replaced by one man's lie.

The cry unheeded.
Now, thousands will die.

Life

Birds are still singing,
Dogs are barking, cats are sleeping.
The tide manages to keep
Rolling in and back out.

Spiders still startle, as they
Appear when you least expect them.
The sun and the moon maintain
Their status above us.

Life continues as we scramble
In fear for our own.
We may disappear, but the birds,
Dogs, cats, tide, spiders, sun, and moon

Will live on.

About The Author

Donald Grant is a husband, cook, cat lover, high handicap golfer, and poet. Usually in that order. Living on the Central Coast of California, most days include a walk along the beach with his wife.

Raised as a military brat, he has lived in various parts of the United States and spent several years in North Africa. During his life he has been an engineer, a minister, and small business owner.

He loves to comment on life and when something attracts his attention, he will add his thoughts to a poem or two.

www.ingramcontent.com/pod-product-compliance
Lightning Source LLC
Chambersburg PA
CBHW060547030426
42337CB00021B/4470